Ultimate Acadia

ULTIMATE
Acadia

50 REASONS TO VISIT
MAINE'S NATIONAL PARK

Virginia M. Wright
Photography by Mark Fleming

All photos copyright 2013 by Mark Fleming
except for the following pages: 98–99 © Wallace
Weeks/Shutterstock.com; 122-123 © Bruce
Macqueen/Dreamstime.com

Design by Miroslaw Jurek

ISBN 978-1-60893-224-5

Printed in the U.S.A.

5 4 3 2 1

Down East
Books · Magazine · Online

Distributed to the trade by National Book Network

Library of Congress Cataloging-in-Publication
Data available upon request

INTRODUCTION

Carved by glaciers, chiseled by the relentlessly pounding surf, Acadia National Park is at once tranquil and wild, changing yet enduring, a place of beautiful contradictions.

One of the smallest parks in the National Park System and the only one in the Northeast, Acadia lies within a day's drive of one quarter of the North American population, attracting more than two million people a year, most of them in summer. Yet solitude is easily found on the 120 miles of hiking paths, 48 miles of carriage roads, and even on the well-traveled Park Loop Road if one ventures out onto the pink granite shoreline and settles on a sun-warmed ledge to watch the crashing waves.

Acadia National Park's roots can be traced to two men who loved the Maine coast and their wish to preserve it for future generations: George Bucknam Dorr and John D. Rockefeller, Jr. Dorr, a Mount Desert Island summer resident in the early 1900s, spent much of his adult life bringing the park into being. Over a period of forty years, he acquired parcels with his own money and persuaded many others to do the same, and he tirelessly lobbied politicians and government officials to give the land federal protection. Among his lasting legacies are the beautiful hand-built stone stairway trails that distinguish hiking in Acadia National Park. Rockefeller, too, gave generously

— indeed, he is the single largest donator of land to Acadia, his gifts amounting to roughly one-quarter of the park's 47,000 acres. Like Dorr, he left an indelible mark on the landscape: his carriage roads and stone bridges are among Acadia's defining characteristics.

For all the spectacles, natural and manmade, that Acadia bestows upon its visitors, there are places of subtler beauty: the Park Loop Road delivers sun-dappled birch forests and expansive meadows; Sieur de Monts Spring gives unexpected insight into the natural world through the Wild Gardens of Acadia and fascinating lessons about Native American culture and history in the Abbe Museum; the carriage roads slip past freshwater marshes, blueberry patches, and peaceful ponds upon which rest beaver lodges and a snapping turtle or two.

You'll find these settings and experiences in *Ultimate Acadia: 50 Reasons to Visit Maine's National Park*. Part thrilling, raw coast, part gently groomed wilderness, all intertwined with quiet lobstering villages and festive resort towns, Acadia is a distinctly Maine treasure.

PARK LOOP ROAD
IS MAINE'S MOST SCENIC DRIVE

What Old Faithful is to Yellowstone, the Park
Loop Road is to Acadia: If you have only
three hours to spend at Acadia, you spend
them here. If you have a week to explore, you
begin your exploration here. And if you're
hiking, biking, rock climbing, riding horses,
or sunbathing, chances are, you get to your
adventure via this avenue. Park Loop Road is
Acadia's premier attraction.

Nineteen years in the building, Park
Loop Road is, in part, philanthropist John D.
Rockefeller Jr.'s creative response to the arrival
of automobiles on Mount Desert Island, a
development he had long opposed (cars were
banned on the island from 1908 to 1915). By
helping to finance the road, he took control of
the inevitable: The cars were coming, but his
motor road would keep them out of the park's
interior and off his beautiful carriage roads. He

did not stint on the design. He hired landscape architect Frederick Law Olmsted Jr. of Olmsted Brothers, renowned for his city park systems, to recommend a route that would take in some of Acadia's most remarkable natural landmarks and create breathtaking overlooks. Rockefeller poured so much money into the project, that locals dubbed it "Rockefeller's Four Million Dollar Road."

It is the ultimate Sunday drive. For the first half of its twenty-seven miles, Park Loop Road unfolds one gasp-eliciting view after another. From the Hulls Cove entrance on the northern end of Mount Desert Island, the roadway traverses the Bluffs with their panoramic views of vast, blue Frenchman Bay, then curves inland to a serene landscape of sun-dappled white birch woodlands, golden meadows, and small ponds.

A few more miles south, the road is shadowed by the dark granite cliffs of 1,058-foot Champlain Mountain. Here people train their binoculars on the Precipice, where hikers negotiate a vertical labyrinth of narrow ledges and rungs embedded in the rock. More tantalizing ridge-top views of the ocean follow before the road drops down to meet that cold blue sea. Waves crash against pink granite cliffs and cobble beaches, whose

smooth stones clink together and sing as the water rushes in and out.

Next the road loops inland to a different landscape entirely. This lush, mature spruce and pine forest was spared by the devastating fire of 1947, which burned more than 17,000 acres on Mount Desert Island in fourteen days. The forest has not, however, been spared winter's powerful winds – it is a forbidding tangle of lichen-draped blow-downs and mossy hummocks.

Now Park Loop Road skirts Jordan Pond and Eagle Lake, offering glimpses of Rockefeller's carriage roads, stone bridges, and carriage houses, then rises once again through newer deciduous woodlands and passes the turnoff to the summit of Cadillac Mountain.

Park Loop Road is a journey through a gentleman's wilderness – a natural landscape tamed to allow people inside, yet preserved to inspire awe and wonder.

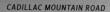

Mile by Mile: Park Loop Road

ANYONE CAN WALK THE OCEAN PATH

As far as Acadia hiking goes, the Ocean Path, a wide, graded, mostly level, two-mile walkway, is for sissies. But for filling one's senses with Acadia's raw, wild beauty, this amble is unsurpassed. Glinting ocean, thundering waves, the intermingling salt and spice of sea and fir – the Ocean Path has it all. Paralleling Park Loop Road, the path takes in several of Acadia's most famous natural landmarks, among them Sand Beach, Thunder Hole, Monument Cove, and Otter Cliff.

SAND BEACH

IS 290 YARDS OF PARADISE...

People often laugh at the seemingly unimaginative name of this little strand, but it does just what a good label should: It distinguishes this beach from any other in Acadia National Park. Sand Beach is the only natural sand beach on Mount Desert Island; the park's sandy beach at Echo Lake, a freshwater pond south of the village of Somesville in MDI's southwestern interior, is manmade. Indeed, natural sandy beaches are a rarity in Maine, whose jagged three-thousand-mile coastline is largely defined by granite boulders, ledges, and cliffs.

A 290-yard, soft, pinkish-white crescent tucked between rocky headlands, Sand

Beach is a carbonate beach, meaning its sand is comprised largely of the finely ground shells of mussels, periwinkles, urchins, and other shellfish, a biogenic composition more typical of the tropics. Washed in by the currents, the sand accumulates in the shelter of Great Head, the rugged promontory at the beach's eastern end, and Old Soaker, an island just offshore.

In winter, however, Sand Beach sometimes defies its name, as storm-whipped waves and winds siphon the sand away, exposing the big rocks underneath. "The sand disappears," Acadia National Park ranger Carmedy West tells people during guided walks on the Ocean Path, "but it always comes back in the spring."

...but it's cold!

The water temperature at Sand Beach rarely exceeds fifty-five degrees, according to the National Park Service.

BAR HARBOR
IS A FESTIVAL ALL SUMMER LONG

Maine's best-known tourist town, Bar Harbor bustles with activity spring to fall. Most of Mount Desert Island's stores, restaurants and hotels are here, and downtown takes on a carnival atmosphere in summer. People crowd the sidewalks, making their way among the boutiques and art galleries, eating lobster and sipping beer at outdoor cafes, and listening to band concerts on the town green.

Incorporated in 1796 as Eden (after English statesman Sir Richard Eden, not the mythical garden), the town renamed itself in 1918 for the sand bar that runs from the shore to Bar Island. By then, the town's golden era as a summer playground for America's wealthiest and most powerful people (J.P. Morgan, George Vanderbilt, and Joseph Pulitzer among them) was beginning to fade.

The fire of 1947, which destroyed hundreds of mansions and cottages and several luxury hotels, dealt the final blow.

Bar Harbor's appeal as a vacation place, howver, has not only endured, but grown. In addition to the millions of tourists who arrive by car, thirty to fifty big cruise ships lay anchor in the harbor each summer.

don't miss

● Crossing the sandbar at the end of Bridge Street to explore trails that loop around forested Bar Island. Wear a watch: You have about an hour and a half before and after low tide to visit; otherwise, you may get stranded.

● Seeing a movie at the Criterion Theatre and Arts Center, a well-preserved art deco-style movie house at 35 Cottage Street.

● Strolling on the 130-year-old Shore Path, a manicured one-mile loop along the shoreline from the town pier to the Bar Harbor Inn to Wayman Lane.

● Viewing thousands of lobster hatchlings, touching sea creatures, and exploring a salt marsh at the Mount Desert Oceanarium, 1351 State Route 3.

● Tasting lobster ice cream at Ben & Bill's Chocolate Emporium, 66 Main Street. Come on, when else will you have a chance to try it?

THE BUBBLES
ARE BEAUTY EMBODIED

The Bubbles at the pond's north end are named for their
distinctive rounded shape and are said to resemble a woman's
breasts (stories abound that they were originally named the
Boobies or the Bubbies). A trail in the gap between North
Bubble and South Bubble is the quickest (and relatively easy)
route to both summits. Bubble Rock, which appears to sit
precariously on the summit of South Bubble, can been seen
from an overlook on Park Loop Road.

YOU CAN DINE
LIKE A RUSTICATOR
AT JORDAN POND HOUSE...

People may arrive at Jordan Pond House with their skin glistening from a heart-pounding bicycle ride "Around the Mountain" or their hair windblown and briny from a morning on Otter Cliff, yet within minutes of being seated on the tea lawn, they feel as casually sophisticated as the rusticators of Mount Desert Island's past. They soak up a serene view of Jordan Pond while sipping tea and nibbling popovers smeared with strawberry jam.

The tradition of tea and popovers at Jordan Pond House, the only restaurant in Acadia National Park, dates to 1895 when Thomas and Nellie McIntire purchased the Jordan Homestead, added birch-wood dining rooms with massive fieldstone fireplaces, and began catering to wealthy summer visitors. The McIntires ran their tearoom for nearly fifty years, after which John D. Rockefeller Jr. purchased the property and give it to the National Park Service.

The McIntires' building was destroyed by

JORDAN POND GATE HOUSE

fire in 1979; a more contemporary version of the Jordan Pond House opened three years later. The Acadia Corporation, the private concession that runs it today, serves an extensive menu of classic New England dishes like steamed lobster dinners and seafood chowder, not to mention a few items the rusticators likely would not have recognized, such as baked brie in phyllo. But Jordan Pond, with the twin mountains known as the Bubbles at its north end, is no less beautiful that it was at the turn of twentieth century.

...and your meal will include these

Popovers can be tricky to bake. The cooks at Jordan Pond House recommend using popover pans, which help circulate the heat around the cooking popovers. A convection oven also can provide proper air circulation.

2 large eggs
1 cup whole milk
1 cup sifted all-purpose flour
speck of baking soda

Preheat oven to 425 degrees. Beat the eggs at high speed in an electric mixer bowl until lemon colored (two to three minutes). At slowest speed, add very slowly one-half cup of the milk; beat until well mixed. Sift and measure the flour, salt, and soda; add slowly (with mixer going on slow speed). When mixed, stop the beater, scrape the sides of the bowl with a spatula, turn to medium speed, and add slowly the rest of the milk; beat two minutes. Turn to high speed and beat five to seven minutes. Batter should be smooth and about the thickness of heavy cream. Pour batter through a strainer, and then into well-greased muffin tins or custard cups. It is not necessary to heat these before using. If a muffin tin is used, fill the end cups and to the top if you wish high large popovers. Bake on the middle shelf of preheated 425 degree oven for the first fifteen minutes. Without opening the oven, reduce the temperature to 350 degrees and bake fifteen to twenty minutes longer. They are best when served at once, but may be kept in an oven for an additional four to five minutes. Approximate yield: 6 large popovers.

RECIPE COURTESY DAVID B. WOODSIDE, PRESIDENT AND GENERAL MANAGER, ACADIA CORPORATION

THUNDER HOLE
THRILLS

Truth be told, most of the time this fissure in a pink granite cliff might best be called Gurgle Hole, so wimpy is the sound it emanates when water retreats from the shallow sea cave just under the ocean's surface. That doesn't stop crowds from gathering on an overlook to watch and listen as the sea rolls mesmerizingly in and out of the narrow cleft.

When the surf is high, they are rewarded with a spectacle of sight and sound: A foaming wave rushes into the fissure with a thunderous clap, spraying water thirty feet into the air.

When Thunder Hole is at its most spectacular, it also can be at its most dangerous. On a warm overcast day in August 2009, the Maine sea was high and rough, stirred up by Hurricane Bill off the coast of Newfoundland. Hundreds of people gathered at Thunder Hole to watch waves smash against the rocks. One powerful rogue wave crashed over a couple dozen people, knocking them off their feet. Eleven people were hospitalized, most for broken bones. Two were rescued; the third, a child, perished.

YOU CAN CLIMB TO GREAT HEIGHTS

There are twenty-six mountains in Acadia National Park, eight of which are over one thousand feet high:

Cadillac, 1,530

Sargent, 1,373

Dorr, 1,270

Pemetic, 1,248

Penobscot, 1,194

Bernard, 1,071

Champlain, 1,058

Gilmore, 1,036

YOU'LL SEE
GREAT ARCHITECTURE
IN THE WOODS

Rockefeller financed sixteen of seventeen carriage road bridges. Built from quarried island granite, each bridge is unique. Bridges built between 1917 and 1928 are credited to architect William Welles Bosworth. The remaining bridges were designed by Charles Stoughton, except for the Triad-Day Mountain Bridge, which was built by the National Park Service.

1917 Cobblestone Bridge. The round boulder facing of this bridge over Jordan Stream is unique in the carriage road system.

1919 Little Harbor Brook Bridge. This forty-foot-long bridge has a single round arch spanning twenty feet.

1920 Jordan Pond Bridge. The 40-foot-long bridge with a large, single arch crosses Jordan Stream.

1925 Deer Brook Bridge. This high, 140-foot-long bridge with two tall, narrow arches crosses Deer Brook near Jordan Cliffs.

1925 Hemlock Bridge. Noted for its massive Gothic arch, the bridge crosses Maple Spring Brook near Hadlock Pond.

1925 Waterfall Bridge. Spanning Hadlock Brook, this bridge has a distinctive pair of semi-circular viewing platforms.

1926 Hadlock Bridge. This small-scaled rough ashlar-faced bridge has a single twenty-foot-span segmental arch.

1927 Chasm Brook Bridge. This is a small-scale ashlar-faced bridge with a single arch and flared deck.

1927 Eagle Lake Bridge. This 118-foot-long Gothic-arched bridge carries State Route 233 over a carriage road.

1928 Amphitheatre Bridge. This soaring, 236-foot-long structure traverses a deep ravine.

1928 Bubble Pond Bridge. This bridge has a distinctive elliptical arch and is rough-dressed in randomly laid rubblestone.

1929 Duck Brook Bridge. This spectacular, soaring three-arch structure, clad in ashlar, has two tall, narrow arches.

1931 West Branch Bridge. One hundred and seventy feet long with a tall narrow arch, the bridge across a ravine formed by Jordan Stream is simply clad in randomly laid ashlar.

1932 Cliffside Bridge. This 232-foot-long structure crosses a deep ravine near the Amphitheatre.

1932 Jordan Pond Road Bridge. The span carries an automobile road over a carriage road near Seal Harbor.

1933 Stanley Brook Bridge. The main arch of this triple-arched bridge spans Stanley Brook Road, which connects Seal Harbor Beach and Jordan Pond.

1938 Triad-Day Mountain Bridge. The only carriage road bridge not financed by Rockefeller, it carries a carriage road over the Park Loop Road.

SOURCE: A GUIDE'S GUIDE TO ACADIA NATIONAL PARK (NATIONAL PARK SERVICE, U.S. DEPARTMENT OF THE INTERIOR)

COBBLESTONE BRIDGE

SCHOODIC PENINSULA

BELONGS TO THE CURIOUS (AND LUCKY) FEW

The Schoodic Peninsula has the distinction of being both the only portion of Acadia National Park that is on the mainland and, after Isle au Haut, the park's most remote section. Only about 10 percent of Acadia's two million annual visitors make the hour's drive east from Mount Desert Island.

With its sweeping views of Mount Desert Island – just four miles away as the crow flies – and the pounding surf at Schoodic Point, Acadia's Schoodic District is high on natural drama, yet a low-key recreational experience. Except for a few hiking trails leading to 440-foot Schoodic Head, the park encourages meandering, contemplative exploration rather than sweaty physical challenges. A six-mile,

one-way loop road, with plenty of turnouts for stopping and soaking up the scenery, hugs the shoreline. A spur leads to Schoodic Point, whose windswept pink granite ledges are laced with black dolerite dikes – magma that filled fractures in the granite thousands of years ago.

In recent years, the Schoodic District has become a laboratory of sorts, dedicated to the study of the natural world. A former U.S. Navy facility has been converted into the stunning seaside campus of the Schoodic Education and Research Center (SERC), whose mission is to advance science and learning. The largest of twenty such centers that have been created in the National Park System since 2003, SERC is raising the profile of this Acadia satellite by hosting a diverse collection of science scholars, from the thirty-five entomologists who spent several days one summer collecting and identifying butterflies to the seven hundred Maine middle-schoolers who conducted biological research in the park.

THE
WAVES
HAVE SCULPTED
NATURAL WONDERS

Monument Cove is a small boulder beach named for its twenty-foot-tall pink granite sea stack. The blocky tower was separated from the adjacent cliffs by wave erosion. The rock walls are riddled with small cavities and overhangs that have made the cove a destination for bouldering.

FLORA AND FAUNA ABOUND

Acadia is home to:

1,101 species of flowering plants

338 species of birds

40 species of mammals

31 species of fish

11 species of amphibians

7 species of reptiles

SOURCE: NATIONAL PARK SERVICE FACT SHEET

THE BIRD-WATCHING
IS FIRST RATE

"Sharpie going fast left!"

"Kestrel right down in front of us!"

"Broad-wing!"

"Merlin coming up!"

The shouts flurry from the eight people sitting on camp chairs on a ledge atop Cadillac Mountain. Their binoculars are trained on "the hole," the narrow, deep gorge running between Cadillac and Dorr Mountain, out of which winged shadows are popping skyward and fluttering in all directions. "It's going to be a rapid-fire day," says Acadia raptor ranger Angi King Johnston.

Acadia is not well known as a wildlife-watching destination. Yes, whales are sometimes spotted off Otter Cliff, beaver dams can be found in many of the ponds, and whitetail deer, once scarce, are now fairly common. But by and large, vacationers don't come to Acadia to see animals.

Unless, that is, they're birdwatchers.

More than three hundred species of birds spend at least part of the year at Acadia, an important migratory bird stopover and nesting site. Birders look for yellow, black-throated blue, and Nashville warblers at Sieur de Monts Spring, and great blue herons, wood ducks, and American black ducks at Bear Brook. But it is on top of Cadillac Mountain that watching birds becomes a mission.

Every day from mid-August to mid-October, volunteers join park rangers at the head of Cadillac North Ridge Trail to count the thousands of raptors making their way south to warmer areas for the winter. Besides informing Acadia National Park about its raptor populations, the data is reported to the Hawk Migration Association of North America, a raptor conservation organization that has more than two hundred hawk-watch sites across North America. There are only two East Coast sites farther north than the one on Cadillac Mountain; both are in New Brunswick. "This site is special because it's the highest point on the eastern seaboard," Ranger Johnston says.

Conditions on this morning in early September are perfect for migration. "We have a north wind, lots of sun, low humidity," Johnston explains. "These birds only fly when conditions are just right. We could have fewer than ten birds on a south wind. We could have more than one hundred on a north wind day."

Johnston has brought along a chart with raptor silhouettes to help visitors identify the birds. As the names of individual species are called out by the watchers, she shares what she knows about them. "Merlins really like to harass other birds up through here, even other raptors," she says when one of the small falcons darts out of the hole.

The Acadia hawk-watch group had counted on average 2,579 birds over the eight-week month period each year for the past sixteen years. More than 5,000 people typically drop by.

The eight volunteers who are counting this morning are dedicated regulars – some of them are locals; some are visitors who plan their vacations around the hawk watch, which begins each day at 9 A.M. and ends at 2 P.M. As the morning unfolds, more watchers trickle in; by 10 A.M., their ranks have swelled to more than twenty-five people. "On a good day like this," a grateful Johnston says, "we need all the help we can get."

THE
PEREGRINE
FALCONS
HAVE RETURNED

The Precipice on the east side of Champlain Mountain is another birding hot spot in Acadia National Park. Peregrine falcons, an endangered species in Maine, nest on the 1,000-foot-high cliff in spring and early summer, thanks to a reintroduction program begun in 1984.

In the early twentieth century, the raptors were a common sight on the Precipice, but they disappeared in the late fifties, as they did elsewhere in the eastern United States, casualties of the pesticide DDT, which thinned the shells of their eggs and kept their offspring from developing. From 1984 to 1986, the Eastern Peregrine Falcon Reintroduction Program released twenty-two captive-raised young birds near Jordan Cliffs. In 1987, one male from the program returned and established a breeding territory near the Precipice. Four years later, he and his mate had the first successful nest at Acadia in thirty-five years. Since then, there have been anywhere from one to three pairs nesting in the park, and nearly ninety chicks have fledged.

THERE ARE
SECRET
BEACHES

It cannot be seen from Park Loop Road,
and there is no sign alerting drivers to it.
Little Hunters Beach is the reward for those
curious enough about the wooden stairway
in the shadow of a spruce forest to stop and
investigate. The staircase, snug alongside
a small stone bridge south of Otter Cove,
descends steeply to a small, sheltered cobble
beach. The rocks are all manner of colors and
they are wondrously smooth, their bumps
and rough edges having been worn away as
they rolled together in waves over thousands
of years. The beach sings like a wind chime
as the ocean washes over and under the
stones, moving them against each other. On
stormy days, their music is almost deafening.
Any day, rain or shine, the beach promises
solitude. A quick stop "to see what's there"
turns into hours as one becomes absorbed by
the rocks' perfect beauty and wondering just
how deep they go.

YOU CAN RIDE THE
CARRIAGE
ROADS,
ROCKEFELLER STYLE

In the early twentieth century, wealthy summer rusticators dominated the social and political life of Mount Desert Island. What they wanted, they pretty much got, and one thing they wanted was a ban on the noisy, smelly automobiles they left behind in the city.

The Great Automobile War, which pitted these millionaires against year-round residents, raged on Mount Desert Island for thirteen years. It started in 1899 when the town of Bar Harbor, then named Eden, placed restrictions on automobiles that were so stringent, they amounted to a ban. Ten years later, the state legislature did impose an outright ban on cars island-wide, but by then public sentiment was shifting, and the ban was repealed in 1913.

Not coincidentally that was the same year that one of the chief "anti-autoists," John D. Rockefeller Jr., began building his automobile-free carriage roads through the

hills and hollows of Mount Desert Island. The twenty-seven-year project resulted in the forty-five miles of carriage roads that lace the forests of Acadia National Park and today are frequented by bicyclists, hikers, and equestrians. (Another twelve miles of carriage roads are located on private land adjacent to the park.)

A summer resident of Seal Harbor in the town of Mount Desert, Rockefeller did not share the temperament of his oil magnate father, according to Acadia ranger Susan Mayne. Where the elder Rockefeller was an aggressive and controversial businessman, the younger Rockefeller – the only boy of five children – was mild mannered. He was not interested in running his father's businesses, but he was drawn to his dad's philanthropic causes, as well as a number of his own. "He also shared his father's love of driving carriages and of building roads," Mayne tells participants on her carriage road tours. "He began sending out agents to buy up land and set it aside. He had it in his mind from the beginning to donate the roads eventually."

State-of-the-art engineering for their day, the carriage roads were built by workmen who inched their way through the forests with axes, shovels, chisels, and mauls. Called broken-stone roads, they have three layers: an eight-inch thick bed of big rocks, four inches of smaller stones, and, on top, a two to three-inch surface of clay and gravel, all packed down by horse-drawn road rollers (in later years, steamrollers were used). They are raised slightly in the center, so water runs off and is channeled away by culverts made of stone. When the roads were new, their surface had a pink tinge, owing to the Cadillac Mountain granite that was used.

The roads were built to follow the landscape's ridges and contours and take advantage of views. Landscape architect Beatrix Farrand advised on planting and placement of native plants to replace those lost during construction. The result is a network of roadways and bridges that are so harmonious with their surroundings that it seems as if nature meant for them to be there.

That is precisely what Rockefeller wanted. To make it so, he directed every detail, from the roughly hewn coping stones that serve as guardrails (locals called them "Rockefeller's teeth") to the stain and paint on the cedar signposts. He is said to have told George Dorr that for all the carriage roads cost him, they might as well have been constructed of diamonds.

Tip for Equestrians

Bicyclists are the primary users of the carriage roads today, but horses and other pack animals are still permitted on all of the roads except the Witch Hole Pond and Paradise Hill loops, and most of the Eagle Lake loop (horses are permitted between junctions 7 and 8). Horseback riding also is permitted within the Wildwood Stables area and on the following unpaved roads: Hio Fire Road, Man O' War Brook Fire Road, Marshall Brook Fire Road, and Valley Cove Fire Road.

THE OCEAN
SERENADES
YOU AS YOU HIKE

The Beehive, a 520-foot-high dome, is a good trial run for the Precipice. It features an almost vertical climb, with rungs embedded in the rock face and narrow ledges that often find hikers hugging the cliff face for security. It comes with a most unusual soundtrack — the crashing of waves on Sand Beach, whose white sand and aqua waters are never out of view.

YOU CAN SLEEP
UNDER THE STARS

Acadia is all about enjoying the natural world, and camping completes the immersion in the outdoors. The park campgrounds are cheap, pleasant, and clean, if rustic.

BLACKWOODS CAMPGROUND

Located a couple miles northeast of Seal Harbor off Route 3, Blackwoods is convenient to trails and carriage roads, and a woodland trail leads to the Loop Road near Little Hunter Beach. 306 sites. No hookups; private showers nearby. Fee: $20/night May 1 –Oct. 31; free, December 1 to March 31. 877-444-6777.

SEAWALL CAMPGROUND

Seawall, located on Route 102A about four miles south of Southwest Harbor, is the campground of choice for those looking to escape the crowds. No hookups; private showers nearby. 214 sites. Fee: $14 walk-in tent sites; $20 drive-up tent, camper, and motorhome sites. Open late May through September 30. About half of the campsites are non-reservable and are sold on a first come, first served basis at the campground. 877-444-6777.

WILDWOOD STABLES CAMPGROUND

Open only to visitors with stock animals, this campground is operated by a private concession, Carriages of Acadia. 10 sites with box stalls. Fee: $15 per night; $25 per horse. Open Memorial Day to mid-October. 877-276-3622.

DUCK HARBOR CAMPGROUND

Located on Isle au Haut, this is Acadia's most remote and primitive campground. There is a composting toilet and hand pump for water. Five sites with lean-to shelters. Party size is limited to six persons per site. Open May 15 to October 15 by advance reservation only. Fee: $25 for special use permit fee regardless of how many nights you wish to camp. 877-276-3622.

BLACKWOODS CAMPGROUND

THE QUIET SIDE
REALLY IS QUIET

Seawall Beach, on what is commonly known as Mount Desert Island's Quiet Side (that is, the island's western half), is a gateway to an entirely different Acadia. There are no rugged mountains and no towering cliffs here; indeed, it is quite flat. The beach itself is a field of boulders, rocks, and granite slabs, millions of which have been pushed by storm surges into a long crest – hence Seawall's unofficial other name, Storm Beach. Route 102A, the only road along this stretch, traverses the cobble ridge, which separates the ocean from a small saltwater pond. Just northeast of the pond is Big Heath, a tranquil 420-acre coastal plateau peat bog favored by bird watchers for its populations of palm warblers, common yellow throats, ospreys, and bald eagles.

Nearby is wooded Seawall Campground, one of Acadia's four campgrounds. On MDI, it is the lodging of choice for visitors seeking solitude and simplicity. "Even on bad days when the fog is rolling in, it has a mystical quality about it," says Ranger Marika Savoy. "It's a beautiful, magical place."

THE RANGERS WILL
ENTERTAIN (AND TEACH) YOU

We know, we know. You're on vacation, and that means freedom from lectures and appointments. But make an exception for a few of the ranger-led programs. They really do enhance your visit to Acadia National Park.

Acadia's rangers offer insight into everything from the critters that make their home on Mount Desert Island to the men and women who created the park. Some of our favorite programs, like Stars Over Sand Beach, Cadillac Mountain Hawk Watch, and the Islesford Scenic Cruise, are featured elsewhere in this book. The following also are well worth your time. For a full list and weekly schedule, pick up a brochure at the visitor's center or campground office or visit nps.gov/acad.

DIVE-IN THEATER BOAT CRUISE. During this three-hour cruise on Frenchman Bay, you watch on video as a diver scours the ocean floor for marine life to bring on board for study.

BEAVERS' WORLD. At dusk, a ranger leads a walk around a pond to look for the critters that build dams and lodges out of branches they harvest themselves.

INTERTIDAL INVESTIGATION. There's a whole world in a tide pool. Rangers explain who's living there.

THE MISSING MANSION. Rangers tell the story of George Dorr, the Father of Acadia, while you explore the site of his estate.

LIFE'S A PICNIC

Of course, you can picnic just about anywhere at Acadia — on the rocks at Otter Cliff, atop Cadillac Mountain, on the beach at Echo Lake. A few places, though, have been specifically outfitted with picnic tables, grills, and restrooms:

- Bear Brook Picnic Area, Park Loop Road, just south of Sieur de Monts Spring
- Fabbri Memorial Picnic Area, Park Loop Road, near Otter Point
- Pretty Marsh, Route 102, on the northwestern side of Mount Desert Island
- Seawall, Route 102A, between Southwest Harbor and Bass Harbor
- Thompson Island, off Route 3, just before crossing from the mainland onto Mount Desert Island
- Frazer Point, near the entrance of Acadia's Schoodic Peninsula section

THAR SHE BLOWS!

Hikers on the Gorham Mountain and other oceanside perches often spot whales surfacing in the distance. You can increase the odds of seeing one of these magnificent creatures on a whale watch cruise. The Bar Harbor Whale Watch Company's high-speed catamaran takes passengers into the Gulf of Maine in search of humpbacks, minkes, and finbacks. The company offers several other wildlife-watching cruises as well, including puffin, seal, and pelagic seabird trips. (1 West St., Bar Harbor. 207-288-2386. barharborwhales.com)

OTTER CLIFF
WILL TAKE YOUR BREATH AWAY

Soaring 110 feet above the sea, Otter Cliff is the Ocean Walk's grand finale. The cliff, a popular destination for rock climbers, is made of Cadillac granite, the distinctive pink rock for which Acadia is known. The cliff and nearby Otter Point and Otter Cove are named – or rather, misnamed – for the sea mink that once swam and hunted in these cold waters, according to park ranger Carmedy West. Prized for their fur, the animals were hunted to extinction in the nineteenth century.

Just offshore of Otter Cliff, a bell buoy clangs above the crashing of waves, warning lobstermen and other boaters of Spindle Rock. At low tide, Spindle Rock's dark humped back emerges like a surfacing whale, but at high tide it is hidden and treacherous. French explorer Samuel de Champlain encountered Spindle Rock in 1604 – with the bottom of his boat. His expedition team towed the boat into Otter Cove for repairs.

You can learn to climb.
Yes, even you!

If the idea of playing Spider-Man on Otter Cliff appeals to you, consider a half- or full-day course with Atlantic Climbing School, based in Bar Harbor. ACS, which boasts that the majority of its students are first-time climbers, offers instruction at Otter Cliff and other sites in the park, including Great Head, Monument Cove, and South Bubble. *Atlantic Climbing School, 67 Main Street (P.O. Box 514), Bar Harbor, ME 04609. 207-288-2521. acadiaclimbing.com*

GREAT HEAD IS NO ORDINARY DAY AT THE BEACH

Great Head, the headland that defines the east end of Sand Beach, is ringed with a two-mile trail — an easy walk except for the short but moderately strenuous hike to the top. Just 145 feet high, the bare, windswept promontory yields panoramic views of Schooner Head and Oak Hill Cliff to the north, Sand Beach, Monument Cove, and Otter Cliff to the south, and the Atlantic as far as the eye can see. The trail passes the foundation of a stone teahouse tower that was part of the 110-acre summer retreat of Louisa Morgan Satterlee, the eldest daughter of financier J.P. Morgan. The estate, which boasted a Beatrix Farrand-designed garden tended by five gardeners, was a casualty of the Great Fire of 1947. Great Head was donated to Acadia National Park two years later.

THERE ARE SEA CAVES IN THE MOUNTAINS

Gorham Mountain is remarkable for its curious geological artifacts – ancient sea caves burrowed in the Cadillac Cliffs 280 feet above sea level. Thousands of years ago, the land here was six hundred feet lower than it is now, depressed under the weight of 2,000 feet of ice. It rebounded after the glaciers melted and retreated. The Gorham Mountain Trail, which leaves Park Loop Road .3 mile after Thunder Hole, offers a moderate, gradual climb through spruce forest, then across a natural granite "sidewalk" to a treeless 525-foot summit. A bronze plaque at the head of the spur trail to Cadillac Cliffs honors "Waldron Bates – Pathmaker." Chairman of the Roads and Paths Committee of the Bar Harbor Village Improvement Association from 1900 to 1909, Bates spearheaded the construction of twenty-five miles of trails on Mount Desert Island.

YOU GET THE LONG VIEW ON
CHAMPLAIN MOUNTAIN

Champlain is best known for the Precipice, the one-thousand-foot cliff that hikers with nerves of steel like to climb. But there are other, less fearsome ways to experience this mountain, including its longest trail, South Ridge. And it is precisely because it is the longest that it's worth doing. The trail is treeless for almost its entire 1.6-mile length, which mean the views of

EVEN
THE CAIRNS
HAVE A RUSTIC
BEAUTY

In addition to blue blazes, Acadia's trails are marked by cairns. Hikers will find both the conical mounds of stones common to trail networks worldwide and, unique to Acadia, Bates cairns. Developed by Waldron Bates around 1900, the Bates cairn is built with four rocks: two large rocks laid roughly a foot apart topped by a flat rock, which in turn is topped by a smaller rock. Some of the cairns in the park are originals, more than one hundred years old.

BASS HARBOR
HEAD LIGHT HAS
STORIES TO TELL

What Cadillac Mountain is to sunrises, Bass Harbor Head Light is to sunsets. Perched on a fir-covered pink granite cliff at the southernmost point of Mount Desert Island, the lighthouse commands a 180-degree view – the Atlantic Ocean to the east and south and Blue Hill Bay to the west. On clear days, when the sun sinks behind Deer Isle, the sky over the lighthouse is a breathtaking blend of purple and orange.

The only lighthouse on MDI, Bass Harbor Head Light draws a couple thousand visitors a day in high season. Many of them will

Bass Harbor Head Light

Established: 1858

Construction: Brick

Tower height: 32 feet

Focal plane height: 56 feet

Optic material: Fourth order Fresnel (1902)

Year automated: 1974

encounter Al Wiberley, an Acadia National Park volunteer guide, who stations himself on the steep wooden stairway that leads to the rocky shore below the tower (the lighthouse itself is not open to the public, a measure of privacy for the U.S. Coast Guard officers who live in the keeper's house). Wiberley answers visitors' questions and shares trivia and stories about the white brick tower, which is one of Maine's most photographed and most painted lighthouses. Its image is even etched into U.S. quarters issued in 2012 under the U.S. Mint's America the Beautiful Quarters Program.

Among his favorite tales is the curse that is said to have haunted this site since 1858, when construction of the lighthouse began. One of the workmen, the story goes, disappeared. The only clue to his fate: a bloody ax found on rocks nearby. A rumor took hold that the man's body – along with his vengeful spirit – was embedded in the walls of Bass Harbor Head Light, a story that gained momentum as the lighthouse keepers and their family members proved to be a hapless lot, prone to keeling over from heart attacks and strokes or driven out of service by debilitating illnesses. The dreadfulness apparently stopped in 1957 when the Coast Guard took over, Wiberley says.

For a more uplifting tale, Wiberley likes to direct the visitor's gaze southwest to Placentia Island, where Art and Nan Kellam lived without running water, electricity, or neighbors for thirty-five years. "It's a great love story – a story about their love for each other and their love for nature," Wiberley says.

When they ventured out on their 500-acre island for the day, the Kellams would leave each other heart-adorned notes about their whereabouts. They did not court company, preferring simply to be with one another. They did, however, have a few friends – lobstermen and artists, mostly – who admired their pluck and protected their privacy.

A few years before Art Kellam's death in 1985, the couple donated Placentia to the Nature Conservancy in exchange for life tenancy. Nan scattered her husband's ashes there, and sixteen years later, her ashes were scattered there, too.

All that remains of the Kellams' life on Placentia, Wiberley says, is memorial plaque placed by the Nature Conservancy, their home's cement threshold bearing the couple's footprints, and, buried somewhere by Nan Kellam a few years before she died, a pair of wedding rings.

THE TRAILS ARE A REAL-LIFE GAME OF CHUTES AND LADDERS

Hikers who have scaled mountains around the world say the trails at Acadia National Park are among the most beautiful they've tread. They are talking not only about the scenery, but also about the paths themselves, many of which have extensive stone stairways and iron ladders and hand holds embedded in the rock.

Most of these trails were crafted more than one hundred years ago by volunteers who formed village improvement societies for that purpose. Notable among them are Waldron Bates, who innovated the use of stairs and rungs on the island's cliffs and steepest slopes, and George Dorr, Acadia's founder and first superintendent, who advocated the construction of memorial paths (individuals who financed a trail could install a plaque honoring a person of their choice) and who built a number of stairway trails leading from Sieur de Monts Spring to the mountain that is now named for him.

The incredible Ladder Trail on Dorr Mountain in particular is a testament to the dedication of those turn-of-the-century trailblazers. It is a stone staircase almost all the way to the 1,265-foot summit (with a few ladders thrown in for good measure). The innumerable steps were cut slopeside from granite. Like most of Mount Desert Island's mountains, Dorr is bald, so the views are panoramic – ocean to the south and east and Cadillac Mountain to the west.

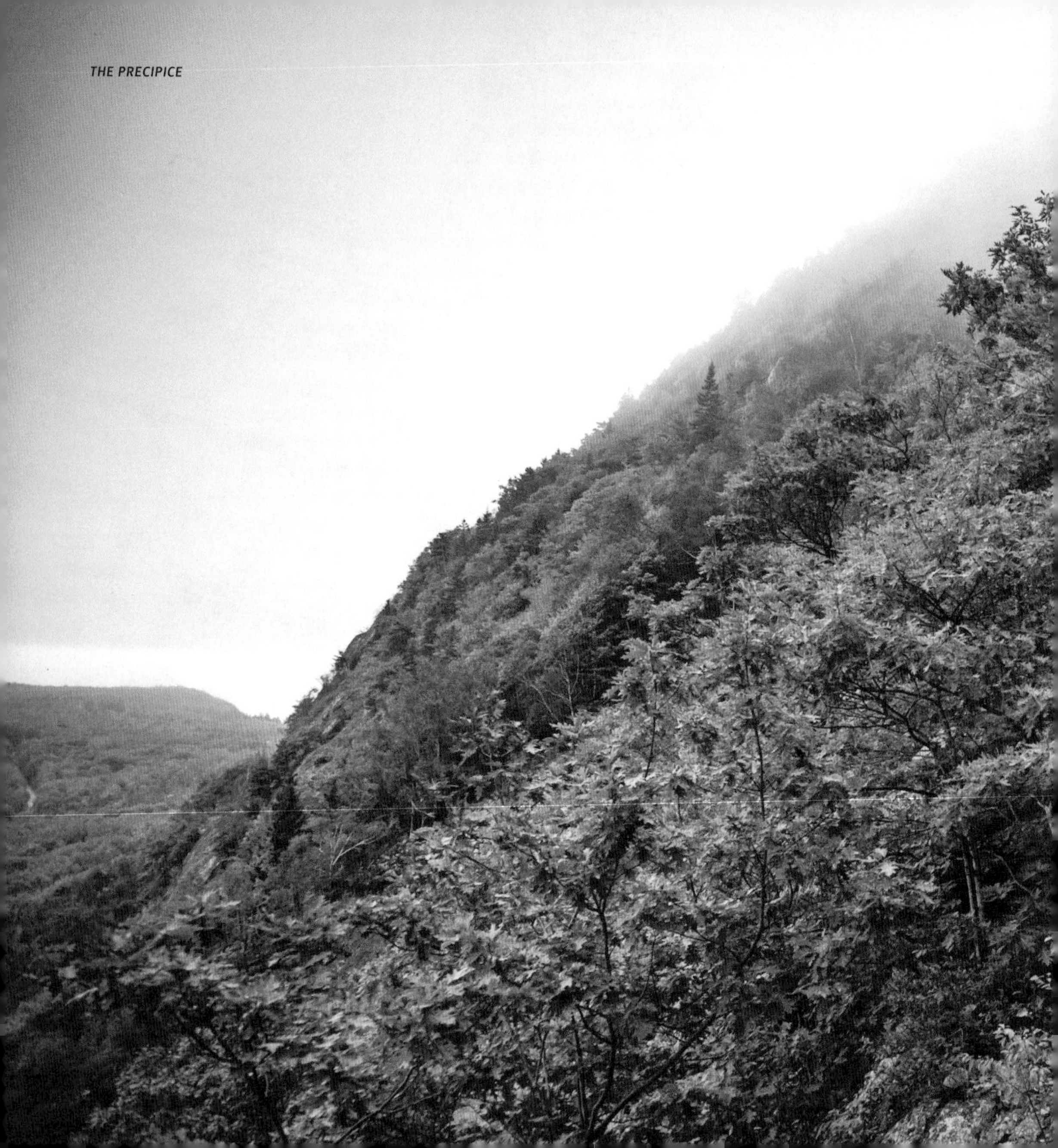

WONDERLAND IS
WONDERFUL.
SHIP HARBOR, TOO

The Wonderland Trail and Ship Harbor Nature Trail near Seawall Beach are among Acadia's easiest walking paths, yet what they lack in mountaintop panoramas, they more than make up for with up-close encounters with the ocean.

Less than a mile long, Wonderland is an abandoned road that passes through a red spruce forest carpeted with sweet and cinnamon ferns. Just before the path reaches the ocean, the woods give way to a rocky outcrop and a grove of pitch pines, gnarled and stunted by the harsh winds, their branches draped in beardlike shrubby lichen. Fragrant rugosa roses edge the pink granite rubble beach, and bald eagles are often seen overhead.

The Ship Harbor Nature Trail is a 1.3-mile loop with interpretive signs whose eastern path follows a narrow and shallow tidal inlet tucked in a thick spruce forest. During the Revolutionary War, an American privateer eluded a British gunboat by slipping into this hidden cove, where it ran aground, forcing the sailors to flee on foot through the woods.

The trail emerges from the trees onto a rugged pink granite shoreline, some twenty feet above the swirling sea. Close to the water's edge the boulders are puddled with scores of tide pools for would-be naturalists to investigate.

Overheard on the Ship Harbor Nature Trail: "This is amazing. This is the best trail I've ever done in all the years I've hiked here."

ON ISLE AU HAUT, YOU FEEL LIKE YOU'RE THE ONLY SOUL AROUND

Isle au Haut is a wild and raw landscape of granite cliffs, rocky beaches, and spruce forests. Owing to its location — six miles off the coast of Stonington — it is by far Acadia's most secluded outpost, accessible only by mail boat or private vessel. About 7,000 people visit each year, and day-trippers are limited to forty-eight at any given time.

Occupying roughly half of Isle au Haut's 5,800 acres, the park has nearly twenty miles of hiking trails, and it is possible to spend a day of exploration here without encountering another soul except on the ferry dock — one in the small fishing village (population: 73) on the northeast side of the island, the other about four miles south at Duck Harbor, where there is a primitive campground with five lean-tos. The paths — over mountains and high cliffs, around marshes, bogs, and Long Pond, and across cobble beaches — are rugged and often wet. They also are absolutely spectacular.

THE MOUNTAINS ARE BALD, SO THE VIEWS ARE GREAT

At just 947 feet, Bald Peak, just north of Northeast Harbor, may not sound like much of a challenge, but in fact, it's a strenuous little hike, all steep vertical rise. As for the name, well, that could apply to almost any summit on Mount Desert Island. Indeed, that is how the island got its name: French explorer Samuel de Champlain, who arrived on these shores in 1604, took note of the rugged treeless hills and named the land Isles de Monts Desert, or "island of bare mountains." The name's French origins are evident in Mainers' pronunciation of the island's name, which places the emphasis on the second syllable: "Mount Dessert."

YOU CAN BAG THREE PEAKS
IN ONE MILE

Just one mile long, the Grandgent trail is one of our favorite hikes, connecting the peaks of Parkman (941 feet), Gilmore (1,036 feet), and Sargent (1,373 feet) mountains. The path is off the beaten path, reachable via the Giant Slide Trail, and it passes through high, open ledges and woodlands, crossing a bog via boardwalk and edging a stream. It's a strenuous trek, with several steep ups and downs, but the views from all three peaks are spectacular.

THE PRECIPICE
IS A GIANT
JUNGLE GYM

PERSONS HAVE RECEIVED SERIOUS INJURIES AND OTHERS HAVE DIED CLIMBING THIS MOUNTAIN.

So reads the sign at the head of the Precipice Trail, the .8-mile ascent (despite its name, this route is not considered by the National Park Service to be a trail, but rather a nontechnical climb) up the one thousand-foot vertical east face of Champlain Mountain. The views of Frenchman Bay from the exposed cliff are stupendous if one dares raise one's head from the matter at hand: first, steep talus boulders, then a series of rungs leading straight up the rock face, narrow stone stairways traversing the cliff edge, and one-foot-wide ledges with nothing but a rebar railing between hiker and drop off.

This route was laid out by Princeton Professor Rudolph Brunnow, whose 1912 brick mansion, Highseas, can be seen from atop Champlain. The manor house now belongs to the Jackson Laboratory, famous for breeding laboratory mice.

THE BOWL
IS PERFECTLY
NAMED

This round glacial pond sits snugly in the basin formed by the slopes of Beehive, Gorham Mountain, and Champlain Mountain. The pond, along with the Beehive, were the first major gifts to the conservation effort that would become Acadia National Park.

SOMES SOUND.
NEED WE SAY MORE?

Nearly splitting Mount Desert Island in half, Somes Sound has fascinated scientists for well over a century. What captures their interest? Defining just what the long, narrow, and remarkably deep body of water is.

Somes Sound is not part of Acadia National Park, but it defines it every bit as much as the Atlantic Ocean does. The sound stretches from the Narrows, a quarter-mile-wide channel between the villages of Southwest Harbor and Northeast Harbor, all the way to the picturesque village of Somesville five miles north. Varying from a half- to three-quarters of a mile wide, the inlet is bordered by granite

walls – Norumbega Mountain (852 feet) to the east and Acadia and St. Sauveur mountains (681 and 249 feet respectively) to the west. Somes Sound is often said to be the East Coast's only fjörd, a steep-sided seawater-filled valley most often associated with the Norway coast, but in fact geologists threw out that label years ago.

A true fjörd, according to the Maine Geological Survey, is several hundred to thousands of feet deep – so deep, that its waters don't mix with the incoming and outgoing tides. Somes Sound, by contrast, is 175 feet deep at its deepest point. Its muddy bottom is well oxygenated, indicating that the water is well mixed.

So, if Somes Sound is not a fjörd, what is it? "It's a fjärd," says Acadia National Park Ranger Bob Thayer, who narrates cruises into the beautiful bay aboard the *Sea Princess* out of Northeast Harbor. "That's kind of like a junior fjörd."

Fjörd or fjärd, Somes Sound is extraordinary.

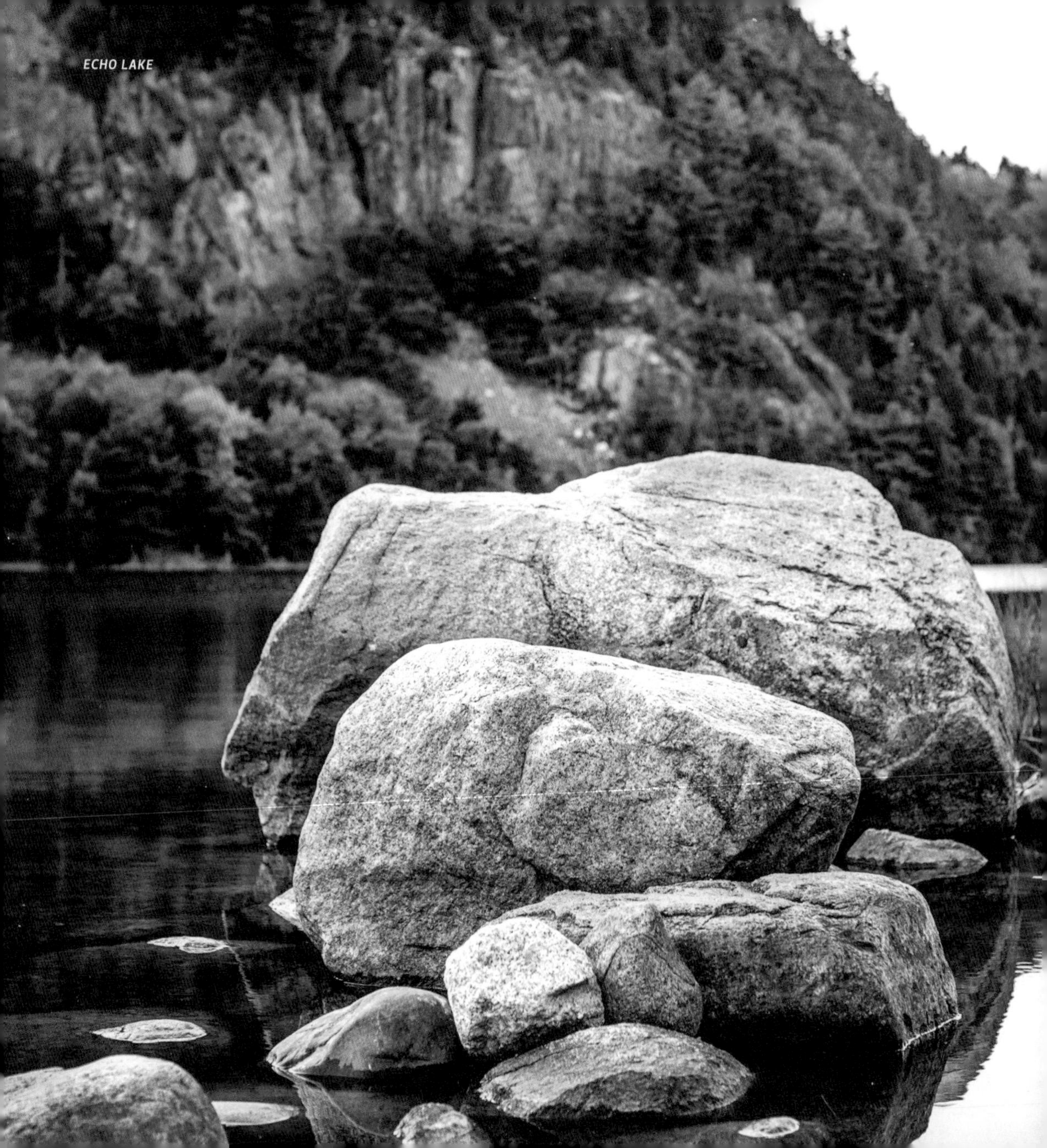
ECHO LAKE

THE QUIET SIDE
HAS GREAT HIKES, TOO

Hiking on the east side of Mount Desert Island is all about ocean views. On west MDI, also known as the Quiet Side, the vistas are filled with Echo Lake, Long Pond, and the incredible Somes Sound.

At 284 feet, Flying Mountain is the smallest mountain in the park, but its granite summit nevertheless elicits sighs. The steep, rocky hill sits snug against the Narrows, the entrance to Somes Sound, affording broad views of Fernald and Manchester points and Western Way beyond. The Flying Mountain Trail descends to Valley Cove, whose shoreline is formed by the sheer slopes of St. Sauveur and Acadia mountains. The water here is so deep, that ships used to anchor right alongside the cliffs to replenish their supply of fresh water from Man O' War Waterfall. As for the name Flying Mountain, according to Acadia Ranger Bob Thayer it comes from a Wabanaki legend that says the hill flew off the summit of nearby flat-topped Acadia Mountain.

One of Acadia's most popular hikes loops over Acadia and St. Sauveur mountains, located just north of Flying Mountain on the western shore of Somes Sound. The trail to Acadia's 681-foot summit is a steep, but fun scramble, requiring some climbing over rocks. The route dips down to the shore of Valley Cove before climbing again to the top of 679-foot St. Sauveur. The views from both summits are splendid: Somes Sound to the east, the Gulf of Maine and the Cranberry Isles to the south, and Echo Lake to the west.

One of the most strenuous climbs in Acadia, Western Mountain has two summits – 1,071 foot Bernard and 949-foot Mansard – and multiple ways to reach them. Both summits are wooded, so the journey is the attraction. The Long Pond Trail follows the western shore of Long Pond and passes through a beautiful birch forest. The Perpendicular Trail to the top of Mansard, by contrast, is another marvel of Acadia trail-building: A moss-covered granite staircase built by the Civilian Conservation Corps in the 1930s, it rises through a cedar forest over the southwest shore of Long Pond.

YOU CAN GET A TASTE
OF HISTORY AT SEA

Every seat aboard the *Sea Princess* is taken as she motors out of Northeast Harbor on her way to the town of Cranberry Isles and a small section of Acadia National Park, the Islesford Historical Museum. About half the passengers on this late summer day are German tourists from an enormous cruise ship that docked in Bar Harbor the day before. Their guide translates as ranger Bob Thayer, standing near the bow with microphone in hand, points out the difference between the lobster buoys and the mooring buoys that bob in the *Sea Princess*'s wake, identifies seabirds flying overhead, spots gray seals and harbor seals, and talks about life on and around Mount Desert Island.

This Islesford History Cruise is the best way to visit the tiny Islesford Historical Museum. It adds depth and dimension to the artifacts of island life that await the passengers, making the journey to and from the museum part of the experience.

Soon the *Sea Princess* is slipping past Bear Island, the smallest of the five Cranberry Isles and home to a couple of cottages and Bear Island Light, which belongs to the park. The lighthouse, built in 1889, was decommissioned in 1981. "There is still a light that shines, but it is not a navigational aid," Thayer says. The task of guiding vessels through the busy intersection of boating channels now falls to the illuminated bell buoy that clangs as it rolls in the swells just off the *Sea Princess*'s starboard side. "It's not as romantic as the lighthouse, but it's a lot cheaper to run."

There used to be three hundred year-round island communities in Maine, Thayer tells the passengers. Today, there are only fifteen, and Little Cranberry Island, also known as Islesford, with seventy-eight residents, is one of them. (Great Cranberry Island, also part of the town of Cranberry Isles, has fifty-one residents.) Its past is preserved in the one-and-one-half-story brick Georgian Revival building that Thayer points out as the *Sea Princess* winds around the lobsterboats in Little Cranberry's harbor and approaches the town dock. Many of the museum's artifacts — old tools, sea chests, historic documents, and family memorabilia — were collected by a cottager named William Otis Sawtelle, who built the museum in 1927 and willed it to the National Park Service. The exhibits include displays on lobstering, whaling, and the U.S. Lifesaving Service, which opened a rescue station on Little Cranberry in 1878.

The island stop is only forty-five minutes, but that's plenty of time to peruse the museum and stroll to the Islesford Market for hot coffee and a square of freshly baked Island Gingerbread. This confection, which curiously enough contains no ginger, is particular to Little Cranberry Island, dating back at least a century when the Woodlawn House hotel served it as "white gingerbread" every morning. Everyone on the island is said to have the recipe, and it has been widely published as islanders share it freely.

Island Gingerbread

1 cup canola oil
1 ½ cups white sugar plus ½ cup for sprinkling top
2 teaspoons nutmeg
1 teaspoon salt
4 cups flour
1 teaspoon baking soda
1 ⅓ cups buttermilk

Preheat the oven to 350 degrees. Grease and lightly flour a 9-by-13 baking pan. In the medium bowl mix together oil, sugar, nutmeg, and salt. Add flour, baking soda, and buttermilk to the mixture. Blend and turn into pan. Sprinkle ½ cup sugar on top of the batter and bake in oven for about 30 minutes.

MOUNT DESERT (THE TOWN) HAS MULTIPLE PERSONALITIES

Wrapping around Somes Sound like a shawl, the town of Mount Desert is comprised of six villages, which can be a bit confusing to newcomers. Some of these villages, like Northeast Harbor, Somesville, and Seal Harbor, have distinct, if small, commercial centers. The largest of these, Northeast Harbor, is frequently mistaken for a town, and no wonder: Southwest Harbor, its counterpart across Great Harbor, *is* a town. Others, like Otter Creek, Pretty Marsh, and Hall Quarry, are largely residential, and their boundaries are fuzzy. It doesn't help that Mt. Desert shares its name with the island over which it sprawls.

Remnants of Mount Desert Island's golden era can be found in Northeast Harbor at two historic gardens managed by the Mount Desert Land and Garden Preserve. Asticou Azalea Garden, an elegant and serene Japanese-inspired landscape, was designed by Charles Savage, the owner of the luxurious Asticou Inn, in 1956. Savage also created the adjacent Thuya Garden, an English-style garden on the former estate of Boston landscape architect Joseph Curtis.

Meanwhile, a new Gilded Age is tucked out of view down the leafy driveways of Seal Harbor. The village is the summering place of some of America's most affluent people, including David Rockefeller, the only surviving child of Acadia's most generous benefactor, John D. Rockefeller Jr., and Martha Stewart, who spends a few weeks each year at Skylands, the fifteen-bedroom estate built for Henry Ford's son, Edsel, in 1925.

don't miss

● Driving on Sargent Drive, a narrow one-way roadway that follows the eastern shore of Somes Sound out of Northeast Harbor.

● Taking a late afternoon cruise into Somes Sound out of Northeast Harbor aboard the *Sea Princess*. (41 Harbor Dr., Northeast Harbor. 207-276-5352.)

● Whiling away a rainy afternoon at the Naturalist's Notebook, a store-cum-museum in Seal Harbor with everything from displays of birds' nests and animal skulls to art supplies to a room that has been transformed into a bat cave. (16 Main St., Seal Harbor. 207-801-2777.)

● Having your picture taken on the gently arching Somesville footbridge, one of the most photographed places on Mount Desert Island.

● Swimming in Echo Lake. The beach on its southern shore is within Acadia National Park.

WHERE ELSE CAN YOU SEE A CROQUET TOURNAMENT?

Named for its location on the southwestern entrance to Somes Sound, Southwest Harbor is to the Quiet Side what Bar Harbor is to west Mount Desert Island – a commercial and tourist center, albeit a much smaller and lower key one. The town is perhaps best known as the home of world-renowned yacht builder Hinckley Yachts, which was founded here in 1928.

Distinguished by cheerfully painted shops, galleries, and restaurants, the downtown is dominated by the elegant Claremont resort, whose leafy campus includes a Victorian hotel with wraparound porch, a smaller inn, and several guest cottages. In August, several dozen people gather on the manicured lawn for the Claremont Croquet Classic, a genteel tournament that dates to 1977. Some of the players have been coming for thirty years.

don't miss

● Cruising into Somes Sound to haul lobster traps aboard the *Elizabeth T.*, a wooden lobsterboat operated by Friendship Sloop Charters. (Dysart's Great Harbor Marina, 11 Apple Ln., Southwest Harbor. 207-460-5200.)

● Paddling with guides from Maine State Sea Kayak. The day's route selection, typically in Western Bay, Blue Hill Bay, or Somes Sound, is guided by weather and tide conditions. (254 Main St., Southwest Harbor. 207-244-9500.)

LOBSTERMEN
STILL MAKE
A LIVING IN TREMONT

The flavor of Mount Desert Island changes dramatically in Tremont. Tourist-oriented businesses and summer mansions are few and far between. The villages of Bass Harbor and Bernard at MDI's southernmost point share a harbor filled with fishing boats, and the docks are piled high with lobster traps and fishing gear. Tremont sprawls northwest to include the villages of West Tremont and Seal Cove, set in a rural landscape of meadows filled with wildflowers

Most visitors come here to see Bass Harbor Head Light, and truth be told, there isn't much else to do but enjoy the stunning views and watch the lobstermen come and go.

don't miss

● Eating a steamed lobster dinner with corn on the cob, cole slaw, and blueberry cake at Thurston's Lobster Pound. The screened-in dining room with the distinctive yellow awnings hovers above the harbor on a long dock. The view is hard to beat. (Steamboat Wharf Rd., Bernard. 207-244-7600.)

● Perusing the antique Cadillacs, Fords, and motorcycles at the Seal Cove Auto Museum. (1414 Tremont Rd. 207-244-9242.)

● Hopping aboard the Swan's Island ferry in Bass Harbor for a day trip to an island community. Bring a bike so you can pedal into the village and down to the square-towered Hockamock Head Light.

THERE ARE
2,600 ACRES
OF LAKES AND PONDS

Blame it on the ocean. Each summer a surprising number of travelers overlooks the park's twenty-four lakes and ponds. These lovely waterways comprise more than 7 percent of Mount Desert Island, yet manage to hide in plain sight, their aquatic splendor overshadowed by the park's bold ocean cliffs and granite-topped mountains. For those willing to venture a few steps off Park Loop Road, these natural gems each offer an experience as unique as the island itself.

ECHO LAKE
Size: 237 acres
Maximum depth: 66 feet
Water visibility: 30 feet

For those seeking a way to cool off during the summertime, Echo Lake, just off Route 102 near Southwest Harbor on the Quiet Side (west Mount Desert Island), offers top-notch, lifeguard-protected swimming. The summertime water temperatures is seventy degrees, rather more friendly to swimmers than Sand Beach, whose ocean waters rarely exceed fifty-five degrees. Families are enticed by Echo Lake's gently sloping sand beach that is ideal for the younger set (older kids may enjoy leaping from the ledges at Ike's Point just up the lake a bit, though rangers urge extreme caution), changing rooms, and the dramatic steep backdrop of Beech and Acadia mountains. A wooden pathway provides a handicapped-accessible entrance to the water.

One of the more interesting features of this area includes the fire tower on the summit of Beech Mountain, a three-story structure first built in 1941 and occasionally open to the public (ask the lifeguards if the Beech Cliffs Trail is open, as it may be closed to protect nesting peregrine falcons).

JORDAN POND

Size: 187 acres

Maximum depth: 150 feet

Water visibility: 46 feet

Most people get to know Jordan Pond from the lawn of the Jordan Pond House, where they sample tea and popovers. But to truly appreciate this gem of Acadia you need to follow the one-mile Jordan Pond Nature Trail around the pond's perimeter. A network of narrow, split-log bridges keeps walkers suspended above the marshy wetlands and allows them to take in the water lilies and schools of golden shiner minnows that fill the shallows. With some of the clearest water in Maine – visibility of up to sixty feet has been recorded here – you might even spot a brookie moving way down deep. Loons and common mergansers nest in this area, and the Jordan Cliffs are home to one of the park's nesting pairs of peregrine falcons.

LONG POND
Size: 897 acres
Maximum depth: 113 feet
Water visibility: 33 feet

As America's second-smallest national park, Acadia can seem a bit too cozy at times, which is precisely when you should venture to Long Pond. The island's largest lake is accessible by dirt road at its south end, or else off Route 102 between Pretty Marsh and Somesville. Here you'll find the wilder side of Acadia, whether you choose to paddle the full four-mile-long length of the pond, take a picnic lunch to Rum Island, or watch the wood ducks feeding in the many coves and inlets. Anglers will particularly enjoy the bass and landlocked salmon stocked by the Maine Department of Inland Fisheries and Wildlife.

A CADILLAC MOUNTAIN SUNRISE IS WORTH GETTING UP FOR...

It is 5:30 on an early September morning and dozens of people are scattered in the twilight among the boulders and ledges atop Cadillac Mountain. Spread out before them is a landscape of lesser hills, the twinkling lights of Bar Harbor far below, and beyond that, the Porcupine Islands enveloped in the meringue of low clouds that blankets the sea all the way to the horizon. The horizon glows rose-pink, and the people watch wordlessly as it brightens with each passing minute.

This is the ritual observed nearly every morning on Cadillac Mountain, at 1,529 feet the highest point on the North Atlantic seaboard, named for French explorer Antoine de la Mothe, Sieur de Cadillac (yes, it is his name on the legendary luxury car – he founded a settlement in the Detroit area). The number of watchers varies dramatically with the season. The road to the summit is closed from December 1 to mid-April; nevertheless,

in all but the harshest weather, someone will be on that mountaintop in the half-light of morning.

The people who have collected here on this chilly late summer morning are rewarded for their patience shortly after six. A pinpoint of glorious light appears on the horizon. Hands move to chests. Breaths intake sharply. Cameras whirr. Over the next few minutes, the light rises higher and wider, and its brilliance is soon too intense to face head on. The whole sky is brighter. Magic moment past, some people now talk quietly. Off in the parking lot a car engine starts, then another, and another, and the watchers begin filing downhill to start the day.

Cadillac Mountain is the first location in the United States to see the sunrise from mid-October to early March. During most of the spring and summer, the sun rises first on Mars Hill in Maine's Aroostook County, about 150 miles northeast of Acadia. For a few weeks around the equinoxes, the sun rises first way Down East at West Quoddy Head in Lubec, the easternmost town in the United States.

. . . *and it's the perfect place and time to pop the question*

No matter the time of year, sunrise on Cadillac Mountain is awe-inspiring, which is why some people choose it as the place to celebrate milestones. Take Henry Hager and former first daughter Jenna Bush. While on vacation in Maine in August 2007, the couple rose at 4 one morning to hike up Cadillac. As the sun peeked over the horizon, Henry dropped to his knee and asked for Jenna's hand in marriage. She said yes.

YOU CAN TRAVEL
TO THE STARS

It's the first night of the Acadia Night Sky Festival, and park ranger Kirk Lurvey is the emcee for tonight's show. A large audience is seated in the darkened house — Sand Beach. Overhead are the players — thousands of stars twinkling against a black velvet sky.

Lurvey, who appears as little more than a silhouette with a dim red tube light around the band of his ranger hat, warms up the crowd. "We'll see planets," he promises. "Maybe some satellites. About thirty of them will pass over our site tonight. And when you see a shooting star, you need to say, 'Oooooooo! Ahhhhhhh!'"

Even with Lurvey speaking into a microphone to hundreds people huddled together on the soft sand, the beach seems enchanted. Waves, barely visible in the infinite darkness, crash and sizzle on the sand. The Milky Way spills from beyond the treetops out over the inky ocean.

This is the largest expanse of naturally dark sky east of the Mississippi, thanks in part to a policy adopted by the National Park Service in 2006 to "preserve, to the greatest extent possible, the natural lightscapes of parks, which are natural resources and values that exist in the absence of human-caused light." The town of Bar Harbor

shares the credit. In 2009, residents approved a dark sky ordinance, which requires new construction projects to install shields on bright lights so that the light is emitted downward.

In October that same year, Acadia National Park, with the help of the Island Astronomy Institute and the Bar Harbor Chamber of Commerce, held its first weekend-long Night Sky Festival with events and workshops related to stargazing. It's now an annual event attracting hundreds of people who attend planetarium shows and lectures at Acadia's Schoodic Education and Research Center (SERC) at Schoodic Point, go on stargazing boat cruises, and gather atop Otter Cliff to admire the moon.

Lurvey spends the next hour talking about the constellations and the Greek myths associated with them. "There is Cassiopea upside down on her throne," he says, pointing at a group of stars with his high-frequency laser. "She thought she and her daughter, Andromeda, were more beautiful than any of Poseidon's nymphs, so Poseidon punished her." He stops in mid-sentence as a light streaks across the sky.

"Ooooo!" exclaims the audience. "Ahhhhh!"

ACADIA FACTS

ACADIA BY THE NUMBERS
Visitors: **2,276,927** per year
Area: **47,000** acres
On Mount Desert Island: **30,300**
Miles of Coastline: **41**
Islands: **16**

NEW GROWTH
The entirety of Mount Desert Island's first-growth forest was harvested by 1870.

MOUNTAIN MONIKERS
In 1918 George Dorr, Acadia's first superintendent, renamed many of Mount Desert Island's mountains so that they would better reflect the history of European exploration. Among the changes: Newport Mountain became Champlain Mountain, Dog Mountain became St. Sauveur, and Green Mountain became Cadillac.

SEE THE LIGHT
Acadia is home to three lighthouses: Baker Island Lighthouse (1828) marks the shoals and ledges around the Cranberry Isles, four miles southeast of MDI. Bear Island Light (1839) is near the entrance to Somes Sound. Bass Harbor Head Light (1858) in the town of Tremont, on the southeast tip of MDI.

WHAT'S IN A NAME
The name Acadia is credited to sixteenth-century explorer Giovanni di Verrazano, who named the northeast Atlantic coast "Arcadia," after the ancient Greek province. The name means "paradise."

HISTORY PRESERVED

There are two museums in Acadia National Park: Islesford Historical Museum on Little Cranberry Island, which documents life on the Cranberry Isles, and Abbe Museum at Sieur de Monts Spring, focusing on the Wabanaki nations.

HIGHS AND LOWS

Acadia is the fifth smallest national park and one of the top ten most visited national parks.

ACADIA: THE APP

Looking for a detailed Acadia guide that doesn't take up a lot of space? Consider *Chimani: Acadia National Park*, a free iPhone and iPad app that provides written and audio descriptions of many of Acadia's features, trails, and activities. Developed by Chimani LLC, the app's data is stored on your iPhone or iPad, so a cell connection is not necessary to access the information. Information is categorized by twenty-nine icons displayed on the main screen. General information includes operating hours, traffic tips, routes for the Island Explorer buses, a calendar of ranger events, and an interactive map. There also are guides for specific activities like hiking, bicycling, bird-watching, fishing, and horse riding. A favorites function allows users quick access to their favorite pages.

Chimani: Acadia is available through the iTunes store.

HIGHEST SPOT

Acadia is home to the tallest mountain on the U. S. Atlantic Coast — 1,530-foot high Cadillac.

FOR THE BIRDS

Acadia is known among birders as the Warbler Capital of North America. More than forty species of warblers are seen here.

BIG ISLAND

Mount Desert Island at 108 square miles is the second largest island on the East Coast of the United States (Long Island is first). Acadia National Park occupies nearly half of it.

UNIQUE POSITION

Acadia is the only national park in the northeastern

1901

Mount Desert Island summer resident George B. Dorr establishes the Hancock County Trustees of Public Reservations, thus beginning a campaign to preserve Mount Desert Island's hills as a national treasure.

1909

The state legislature bans cars on Mount Desert Island, putting muscle behind prohibitions already in effect in Bar Harbor (then called Eden) and the town of Mount Desert.
Dorr buys Sieur de Monts Spring and encloses it in a springhouse modeled after one he saw in Europe. He carves "The Sweet Waters of Acadia" on a nearby rock.

1914

Dorr writes Rockefeller about their mutual interest in protecting land on Mount Desert Island for public use, beginning a lifelong relationship between the two men who would bring Acadia National Park into being.

1908

The Trustees acquire Cadillac Mountain.
Eliza Homans of Boston gives the Trustees their first significant gift, the Beehive, a small but steep mountain near Sand Beach, as well as a nearby round pond known as the Bowl.

1913

At the request of Bar Harbor voters, the legislature repeals its Mount Desert Island automobile ban. Automobile opponent John D. Rockefeller Jr. begins constructing motor-free carriage roads along Little Long Pond and Barr Hill on his Seal Harbor property.

1916

The Sieur de Monts National Monument, encompassing about six thousand acres around Sieur de Monts Spring, is established. Dorr is appointed its first superintendent. He is paid one dollar a month.

1918

The town of Eden changes its name to Bar Harbor.

1922

Construction of the Park Loop Road begins. Locals called it "Rockefeller's $4 Million Road."

1927

The heirs of Wall Street financier John G. Moore donate land at Schoodic Point, notable for its spectacular surf and granite headlands, to the Hancock County Trustees of Public Reservations. It is to be used for a public park and promotion of scientific research.

1930

Rockefeller resumes construction of the Amphitheatre carriage road.

1919

President Woodrow Wilson signs legislation changing the designation of Sieur de Monts National Monument to Lafayette National Park.

1924

Rockefeller halts construction on a carriage road through Amphitheatre Valley after it is vehemently opposed by Philadelphia lawyer and Northeast Harbor summer resident George Wharton Pepper. Pepper says the valley between Cedar Swamp Mountain and Jordan Ridge is one of MDI's most wild and beautiful areas.

1929

Lafayette National Park is renamed Acadia National Park. The Schoodic Point land is added to the park. It is the only portion of the park that is on the mainland.

1941
The last link of Park Loop Road is completed.

1960
John D. Rockefeller Jr., the largest contributor of land to Acadia National Park, dies. His gifts included 15,000 acres, 45 miles of carriage roads, 16 stone bridges, and 2 carriage houses.

1931
Eight hundred cars drive the newly constructed road up Cadillac Mountain, at 1,532 feet the highest point along the North Atlantic seaboard. The road officially opens the following year.

1944
George Dorr, the father of Acadia National Park, dies at the age of ninety-one.

1982
A new, larger Jordan Pond House opens.

1943
About three thousand acres on Isle au Haut are donated to Acadia National Park by the heirs of the founder of a summer community established there in the 1880s.

1947
A fire that began in Dolliver's Dump at Hulls Cove scorches ten thousand acres in Acadia National Park and destroys 170 homes, 77 cottages, 5 luxury hotels, and the Jackson Laboratory. The fire brings Bar Harbor's golden era, already on the wane, to a close.

1932
John Richardson of Topeka, Kansas, becomes the first person to ride a bike up Cadillac Mountain.

1979
The Jordan Pond House is destroyed by fire.

1988

FOA's first fundraising campaign raises $25,000 to restore Bear Island Light.

1999

FOA launches the Island Explorer bus system to relieve traffic congestion in the park and on Mount Desert Island. Eight propane-powered bus routes link hotels, inns, and campgrounds with destinations in the park and neighboring villages. The fare is free. FOA founds Acadia Trails Forever with a $5 million gift from Ruth M. and Tristam C. Colke Jr. The program supports maintenance of Acadia's 120-mile trail system.

2003

Acadia National Park reopens the Homans Path on Dorr Mountain. The trail was built by George Dorr to honor Eliza Homans, who donated the Beehive and the Bowl. It had been abandoned since 1941.

1991

FOA launches a campaign to raise funds for repair and maintenance of Acadia's carriage roads.

1986

Friends of Acadia (FOA), a citizen organization whose mission is to preserve and protect the park, is founded.

1996

FOA's Carriage Road campaign ends. It raised $5 million in endowed funds to maintain the roads in perpetuity.

2002

L.L.Bean pledges the first in a total of $3 million in grants for the Island Explorer buses.

2006

A series of earthquakes on Mount Desert Island cause extensive rockslides on the Precipice Trail and East Face Trail on Champlain Mountain and on the Homans Path on Dorr Mountain. The Homans Path and Precipice were reopened the following year, the East Face Trail in 2008.

ACADIA TIMELINE